Death
And Other Speculative Fictions

An Essay In Prose Poems

Caroline Hagood

SPUYTEN DUYVIL
New York City

For Trish and Louis

For Max, Layla, and Adriel

Nothing of what is born dies, but one thing separated from one part and added to another produces different forms.
    —Anaxagoras

I've seen things you people wouldn't believe... Attack ships on fire off (the) shoulder of Orion... I watched C-beams glitter in the dark near the Tannhäuser Gate. All those moments will be lost in time, like tears in rain... Time to die.
    —Roy Batty's last words in Blade Runner

Though I am long dead as you read this, explorer, I offer to you a valediction. Contemplate the marvel that is existence, and rejoice that you are able to do so. I feel I have the right to tell you this because, as I am inscribing these words, I am doing the same.
    —Ted Chiang, *Exhalation*

I.

DEATH AS THE ULYSSES OF DESPERATE HOUSEWIVES

II.

DEATH AS THE BEGINNING OF *DRACULA*

III.

DEATH AS *FURIOSA*

I.

DEATH AS THE ULYSSES OF DESPERATE HOUSEWIVES

1.

All I want to do since losing my father is molt in my nest while drinking speculative fiction that goes down like a shot of witch tequila. When they all asked if there was anything they could do, I requested a time machine. Back to the future. The piece in the science section recently showed these phenomenally layered images. Some were of planets far away, some of miniscule things seen under a microscope, but both looked the same. A microscope lets us see in miniature, a telescope aimed at space shows us the past, just think what we could do with the DeLorean. Or with language. I've had one too many and I'm ready to remake the spatiotemporal order. I'm shotgunning coffee and Googling, *but seriously how real are ghosts actually?* at three a.m. Then worrying the algorithm will compute this and send me the wrong kind of ghosts.

2.

What have I become? Binge-reading about death at all hours in some off-road attempt to bring my father back from the dead. Is that what this is? In my late-night research, I discover crucial death-related tidbits about the cast of *Jersey Shore* and other deeply important celebrities. For instance, Snooki is very sensitive because she won't eat lobster since they go live to the boil. It's also central to know that Ke$ha is all for donning roadkill and signs off ahead of time in the case that you'd like to wear her teeth as a necklace to the VMAs. I picture that my dad can still see me. He knows I'm working hard to exhume him. He has a wicked sense of humor, and I can feel him in stitches. I got it from him—this dark comedy, investment in haunted things, connoisseurship of the absurd. The more I read, the more I see that the history of writing is the history of grappling with death. Immersing myself again and again in my dad's final moments as I write, edit, and reorder this document; delete and then resurrect sentence fragments, move phrases from here to there, building word by word a linguistic time machine to bring him back to me. I love you, my father. This book is a séance.

3.

My father is across from me, our mouths flapping, into the second hour of talking about *Blade Runner*, when he passes me a dragon fruit. Because I'm revising, I move this here, after he has already died, time machine that is writing, so he can live again on a page, his ghost inflaming the paper's cellulose fibers with its speculative innovations. I also employ computer generated imagery here to make him dance to Bluegrass one last time, look how he moves, jovial, finally at large. One not fun part of revision is having to relive the moments of hope that I only now know were not symbols of his future salvation. But even this revision is an important part of the mourning process, a repetitive exercise in sorrow that eventually alleviates it or, better yet, one supernatural day transforms it into something more audacious. A second—paper—life for my father. How did I get like this? Well, I was an English major for starters. You know the type. In college I thought I could feel the books living inside me. One of the things that starts to happen as you get older, and particularly in this month in which everyone I know is dropping like flies, is that the once clear line between life and death starts to seem more permeable. As my mom says, my father is now everywhere and nowhere. He was so mystical and his sensibility so slapstick, I'm almost disappointed in him for not reincarnating as a wisecracking parakeet or enchanted umbrella.

4.

My dream-obsessed father pretty much only inhabited virtual worlds. How on earth can a guy like that ever be gone? It's just so unimaginative. So not him. Therefore, I conclude it was not my father who died but a dull impostor. But then in which virtuality is he hiding, just waiting for me to find him? Why didn't I see this earlier? Clearly, I have a lot of work to do. Because of what *Ulysses* meant to us, I am now Stephen haunting the streets of Dublin, but in this version of the story, he's my actual father, he's no longer alive, and I know I'll find him in later scenes. So, I just keep walking until my feet grow blood-red, and that's my version of Homer's wine-dark sea that my father and I used to swim in together. But I suppose for now this book will have to be an afterlife of sorts for him. Because in the parts I worked on this morning, my dad hasn't died yet, this is my time-traveling way of undoing his death. I read over these sections where he still lives as though I can go back and inhabit that time. This is called reading. This is called writing. It's why it always feels so ghostly and why all writers are mediums, talking daily with the deceased, resurrecting, bringing back ghost truths from the underworld. Hocus pocus.

5.

So many of our speculative tales are about time and processing our unthinkable histories. In Charles Yu's *How to Live Safely in a Science Fictional Universe*, everyone has and is a time machine, and time itself is also portrayed as an—often malfunctioning—memory-producing mechanism. People's time machines often break down and loop. Luckily, the metafictional main character, also Charles Yu, is a time machine mechanic. Trouble is: this metafictional main character over here (that's me) is not.

6.

What is time, anyway? I mean, they told us something about it, but I distrust it. Instead, I regard an eruption of temporalities spreading on the horizon, a choose your own adventure story. All my favorite writing tells time and space: be gone, or at least as they were. I want them to unmake and then remake themselves right before my staring eyes. I'm making a list of key talking points in case I ever get to speak to my father again. You never know. I start to make out a whimsical frequency I'm hoping might be my dad, but before I can investigate, I crash face-first into bed. I hope my father can find an after-life inside me. And I don't mean "in my memories," but I mean literally build a city out of my ribs and make garbage can fires at night to keep himself warm. I hope he can roast marshmallows there. Then, every time I want to talk to him, all I must do is call down my windpipe, tell him what I'm making, and prepare for his exegesis. Confess to him that, after he passed, I tried to make his Eggs Benedict, but it was more like scrambled eggs because the sauce curdled.

7.

Just in time, the alarm lets me know I'm alive, blasting the early morning to bits. My hand breaks free from covers to fumble for the offending device that's exploding my night world with telephonic gateways into various day-complexities. Every night I sleep and forget. Each morning, I awaken, and my father dies again as I remember. I find my computer by touch. As the portal opens, I feel my rational mind swim off. Nalo Hopkinson says, *the Web is just another threshold between one world and another.* My eyes focus on a screensaver of nature while living in the city. My computer, since being updated, has garnered a brand-new introductory image that I have not selected and it's just one more virtual world, one more speculative fiction, baffling and beyond my control. It's the view from the top of a mountain. Everything is brilliant, green and I remember how I live in a dead cement isle, surrounded by people who don't have enough in one of the richest cities in the world. I cook food to bring them on my way to teach. It's not huge but it's something.

8.

Each day as I make my way to the college, I watch commuters step over people sleeping on the subway platform like they were plastic bags. My heart breaks a little each day and I spend some time every evening rebuilding it, using various pieces of food from the subway tracks. I believe this makes me more open to various perspectives, that such a central organ of mine is constructed from countless pieces of city refuse, all with different backstories, colors, and textures that look the same under a telescope or microscope. If you were to reach out right now to stroke my heart, for instance, you would find something startling—a kitchen. If you look at it from far away, though, it resembles a broken-down city. There was talk of gut-renovating it after the tourists stopped coming but this was soon forgotten. Now, pretty much the only person who touches it is me, and I think it's better that way. But I still leave the side door open.

9.

Speculative fiction asks that we think beyond earthly terms, but since death occurs beyond those terms, it turns out that not only dragon stories but all scientific, philosophical, and religious theories about what happens after we die have been speculative fictions all along. Death in the key of speculative fiction turns *it will end* into *it may end.* These are some odds I can live with. After getting out of the shower, I draw too close to the mirror and ask what is, disappointingly, only myself with a towel turban and nothing more extraterrestrial: *What if the truth of what happens after death could be discovered and it turns out to be world-bending?* In this bent world, I speculate about seeing my father again, or at least on his having multiple marvelous options. I envision him dream-galaxy surfing or becoming the metaphysical librarian of a new strain of beings who actually greatly revere librarians.

10.

Now, as I read reams of writings on human expiration and its many virtualities, I survey the various stances; these writers have been in love with death (many seeming to literally want to have relations with it, until I get it—to many death is sexy), despised it, seen it as their best spiritual and philosophical advisor; but it came for them all regardless. Fascinating in these readings: the romance of death—how it can seem loyal, dependable, a lover who doesn't stray because it will always be there in the end, something that originates in you at birth, which continues to happen to you all your life, and in all these ways it's not strange but all too familiar. That maybe even death is life. Or death is you. Oh no, this will not be a cheery book but, bizarrely, it also will. See how both extremes can be true at the same time so your mind must expand to embrace the unthinkable? Well, that's good training for death. I've gotten to a point where I live in nothing but speculative fiction. I've left the realist world behind altogether. I don't relate to it. It means nothing to me, all those congested highways.

11.

Perhaps I'll be a good sport about dying. I mean, I doubt I will but who knows. A core Pythagorean belief is that souls are reincarnated after death. Once, upon seeing an animal being beaten, Pythagoras defended it, claiming he recognized the soul of an old friend. If I were to go to an after-life store for my dad, I'd order him whatever the people in the movie *Everything Everywhere All at Once* had, with their ability to parallel universe and genre hop. I guess death will be like all the other events I knew would happen in the future, and I just got there and marveled at the eeriness. *Here I am in this surreal moment I thought I'd never live through.* I can't remember my own birth, but the birth of my children was like that, and I believe my own death will be like that too. I'll want to tell everyone, *look at me over here dying, it's wild, can you even believe it?* But who will be able to hear me once I'm in a space only speculative at that point?

12.

Surprise! I'm not writing that thousand-page novel about the intersection between war, commerce and American history that tells the United States back to itself, helps it understand simultaneously where it's been, where it is, where it's going, that I set out to write. Claire Vaye Watkins wrote a whole essay on this tendency of women writers to pander to men in this way, aiming to write *Great American Novels* that will be called *masterpieces* rather than what will inevitably be called *chick lit*. But maybe the most radical thing I can do at this point is resist that, run in the other direction: place on your bed one hot midnight a book with pieces of recipes in it, but, like, recipes for how to turn into a renegade poem or how to literally marry a paradox, with monsters that are real, and a protagonist's journey so deep into the twisted guts of a tampon box that I come out with its ontology. I'm the Ulysses of desperate housewives.

13.

For instance, I'm currently procrastinating the writing I want to do by using Google translate to decipher recipe websites in foreign languages. Please organize an intervention. But food can also act as inspiration. Bram Stoker wrote *Dracula* after a nightmare induced by eating too much crab at dinner the night before. So I'm eating lots of crab as I write this in the hopes that vampires will sneak into the margins. But my father is still dead. Death is no fun, so my new way of managing grief is cooking ornate recipes while listening to audiobooks with structurally rich plots until the two narratives fuse into startling new storylines. As an example: the combination of N.K. Jemison's *The City We Became* and tamales morphs into the tale of how one man gave birth to a city made of masa and either corn husks or banana leaves.

14.

I've been sneaking away to rewatch *The Bear* so I can pause it and write down all the cookbooks on the shelf, and for that instant when Sydney looks at buildings to ponder the architectonics of food-making. Every night I'm staying up late watching Mashama Bailey deconstruct Southern cooking, the Korean Vegan weave lyric essays over Kimchi Jjigae, Michael Twitty reinvent identity by way of Jewish and African American foodways. I could bore you to death with the links between meal prep and outlining, mise en scène and mise en place, setting the scene, but I'll spare you. In terms of what cooking has to say about innovation in writing, though, I will say that yesterday I made Pad Thai but didn't have peanuts, so I used cashews instead, and it came out one hundred percent better.

15.

So now I craft a plan to burrow deeper into the domestic as speculative fiction. In *Like Water for Chocolate,* Tita puts her emotions as magic into the food, causing things to happen. I have always wished to connect cooking with witchery. What is a pot but a cauldron? Were the witches in *Macbeth* braising potatoes where they were boiling toil and trouble? Who's to say? You can see the slippage here. As a child I inhaled the *Mrs. Piggle-Wiggle* series, thinking her witchy, doling out potions from her upside-down house. But maybe she was actually anti-witch because she used her spells to get kids to behave, sapping the wildness. So many childhood enjoyments are like this, retrospectively problematic. Can this analytical adult mind travel back in time and ruin the party? Not really. Anyway, it's all too much, so I cook. I believe the necessary gesture to cope with this shitshow called being alive (or dead) is an impossible one: a simultaneous holding on so tight and letting go, much like the poetics of parenting or poaching an egg.

16.

Understand my unhinged plan: I will be like Tita in *Like Water for Chocolate* and put into a cauldron my wild wish to have my father back, until my dinner becomes necromancy under my mad direction. Not that my son knows I'm having these thoughts, or maybe he does, since he often claims he can read my mind. In a carefully choreographed routine, I take the food from the refrigerator, get the recipe, help him but step back, the motions much like mothering, as I try to simultaneously hold on and let go—Naomi Shihab Nye in her poem "Making a Fist," opening and closing her hand after all those years to see if she's still alive. In Nye's poem, the seven-year-old speaking experiences her first sense of life leaving her, just North of Tampico, riding in the back of a car, her mother in front. So, she asks how you know if you're going to die. Her mother answers, with an odd certainty: *when you can't make a fist anymore*. So random and wonderful that answer. It's hard to read it without reflexively seeing if you can still do it—if you're still alive. In the next stanza, the perspective shifts. She tells us that after all this time, she's alive but still back there, opening and closing her fingers, pondering the melancholy borderlines we must each move through alone.

17.

Xerox this and hang it in the dystopian end-of-world camps: we must work on our apocalypse skills. After seeing *Triangle of Sadness*, and how all the privileged people didn't know how to do anything when stranded on the island, I am happy I have my single practical skill. I will have something solid to bring to the final days. Being able to feed people is not nothing. You might even say it's everything. Cooking can always be used. Saved recipes as autobiography: pesto chicken with a side of world suffering. There's nothing other than this: I take the herbs out of the fridge and pluck them. Then my son takes his five-bladed scissors and starts to flurry the green. We stand next to each other, only time and plant-life between us, basil falls from us, around us, then seemingly through us. He lays the chicken down away from him into the oil, but only, as I've taught him, after it starts to shimmer. I grind the spices with my mortar and pestle. What comes out is, instead of pesto chicken, a transformed multiverse that invites us in. Zeroing in on all that matters: we don't summon my father, but we do eat together at the kitchen island, still talking, edges of our elbows touching on granite, hot basil oil dripping down our chins.

II.

DEATH AS THE BEGINNING OF DRACULA

Two Weeks Earlier…

1.

I'm at my daughter's school. That sound is my mother calling to say my father's in the hospital again after a new treatment for what the doctor refers to as his *rapidly reproducing* cancer. Can I come with the kids tonight? Of course. It's serious. Everything stops. It's Wacky Wednesday at the school, a day to boost the spirits of children who are still figuring out how to be human as we all are. My daughter has made herself a homemade cape out of paper and wears a pink bunny-ears headband with parts that hang down. When you squeeze each side the opposite ear lifts to hear the music of the world. She wants me to look wackier, so I agree to wear the purple paper wings she has made me, even though all the parents look up as the middle-aged fairy walks into the schoolroom. After I speak to my mom, I stand perfectly still, tears forming, in my fairy costume. I close my eyes. I'm a fairy crying in public. A scholar of humiliation. I open my eyes to what I believe to be snow outside the class window. But because the world's conceptually afire, I'm unmoved by these frozen cloud water droplets and their supersaturated air masses. No, that's a lie. I still find a way to be awed. I want to tell these flakes with their delicate sixfold symmetry to fuck off. Instead, I politely inform them in my head that they are splendid because I can't seem to be discourteous even to snowflakes. After all, the snow will turn to rain, transform like all things, end, begin again.

2.

Wait, no. It's not snow. It's a white flowering tree outside the window, I realize as I leave thoughts of snow behind. The miracle treatment didn't work but rather triggered what the doctors are calling a cytokine storm inside my father. It's raining hard out there. Storm outside. Storm inside. He also has Pneumonia. His body, the doctors tell me, once I take the train up, is failing him from various angles. It is shutting down. Mount Sinai is the biblical space of divine revelation, so my father, mother, daughter, and son, together we wait. He has been intubated, tubes snake around him, a bloody port in his neck. He's unconscious, one cyclopean eye ajar but unseeing, still green but clouded. I stare into it for hours, wondering if he can see me. We sing to him all day, rub his feet, hold his hands, kiss his scratchy cheek. The intubation process has knocked out all but two of his front teeth. I run my tongue over my own to see if my fangs are still there. How can they have taken the teeth of the one who made me but left me mine? I wonder if I will start being less afraid of everything now that I've looked into the eye of death. When I see anything so desolate I need to go there. But not this time.

3.

One day they say they're going to take out the breathing tube and wake him to see if his brain still works. I hold and hold him, rub his feet, sing to him. It brings me back to the early days with my children, the simplicity of contact. They don't tell you that you will parent them in the end. It's circular and love-heavy. Strangely satisfying. Also heartbreaking. In Ray Bradbury's "Dandelion Wine," Douglas's great-grandmother, on her way out, tells him she won't ever die because she has a family; that it's not her there with him dying because she's elsewhere looking back at herself, cooking dinner, or reading in the library. Again, this play with time brought on by the specter of death. My father is struggling. Organs failing. They try to take out the tube, but he gets angry and bites them, so they put these white gloves on him. To get through his various hospitalizations, my father thought of himself as the boxer from the Simon and Garfunkel song, and here he lies with his white mitts. It's amazing a whole life comes down to this. All I want to do is tell him about these days. Tell him about the white mitts. But I don't think he can hear me anymore.

4.

He's gained forty pounds of water weight because his kidneys aren't working, and I hold his swollen hand for hours, just like I used to. But this time his hand's something other than a hand, a horror movie limb. But maybe I can reverse this, cause my mind to move in a different direction. What if I were to see it as something audacious that exceeds a hand? What if I were to see death as the most gorgeous part of life? Or, more particularly, as something audacious that exceeds life? I'm not sure I'm there yet but that's the conceptual goal: to be able to soft-shoe right into death's arms, eyes wide, taking it all in, transformed at last by that forbidden knowledge. But who's big enough to really do that? The doctors tell us constantly that he's *not out of the woods*. Well, of course not. He's practically catatonic. He is the woods, or as speechless. When they say it, I imagine various fairytale creatures who have found their narrative meaning in the forest. Is my father's story almost over?

5.

Of all the sick ironies, today is his birthday. My mom and I sing with terrible voices, loudly into his ear at the same time, really not much of a gift to him, but we mean well. She gets him this big balloon shaped like a crown that reads *Birthday King* because I tell her it will cheer him up, if he can still see out of that one ever-ajar eye. Elisabeth Kübler-Ross, who wrote the book that gave us those stages of grief (denial, anger, bargaining, depression, acceptance—ideally), told her kids to release balloons when she died because she considered death to be a graduation. I don't suggest the balloon to my mom for this reason. I'm hoping, as with everything I do around this time, that it will make him live. That birthday king balloon will still be hovering there after they come to take his body away from us a week later.

6.

They're giving him an MRI today to see if there's anybody in there. I can't help but think of the world of ideas we've shared, the brain we've co-owned, and I visualize this co-piloted piece of machinery sliding down a ravine somewhere. Now, the neurologist comes in and asks him to squeeze his hand and wiggle his toes, and he does both. So his cognition seems better, but it turns out he has a new strain of pneumonia, which causes his blood pressure to drop. I've gone so overboard trying to make it not traumatic for my daughter that at first she doesn't seem to realize my father's sick, or involved in this weekend at all. She keeps screaming, *girls weekend,* because my son is on a chess trip. While they talk to me about my father, our magical friend Jeanne takes my daughter to the hospital recreation center, where my girl lines up all the stuffed animals at the table to make it look like they're having a board meeting. The animals are discussing if her grandfather will die. My mother photographs it and sends it to the woman who runs the center to show her how much joy her granddaughter has found there. The woman surprises us by writing back thrilled and not offended by how my daughter has commandeered the space, used it to create a kind of corporate improvisation on dying. Later, my daughter corrects me. They aren't businesspeople. They are doctors in a meeting. And they are not discussing whether her grandfather will die but how to make him live.

7.

At one point, the nurse who manages his tube does something to it, and my father opens his eyes and gasps like a fish in agony repeatedly. There's the story of Jonah and the whale, there's Ahab and his maritime obsession, but what happens when your father, the man who taught you how to ride waves with fearless abandon, becomes a pained fish before your eyes? My mother actually starts crying and she's such a tough one. I of course am also crying but that's not rare. My eye folds have become so enlarged in the past couple days from sobbing that I resemble a puffer fish, and consequently feel more connected to my fish father. I assure myself we are speaking the language of aquatic life together in the hospital. Maybe this conversation will provide the key to how to find him if I lose him. Where will he be? If it's an obvious place, I want to go there and bring him back. I need to learn to locate him on some other plane, but how? Maybe the ocean has something to do with it.

8.

They finally successfully take the tube out and get him off the Fentanyl and we play his favorite, *Parsifal*. I keep repeating like an idiot how Easter is coming and it's a time of rebirth, like saying it will cause him to live until then. My mom and I are arguing about whether he wants to hear Simon and Garfunkel's *The Boxer* or not, so I ask him. He nods and we look at each other as though he is a miracle. I go out to the vending machine and choose a candy to cheer us up. If only we could make similar vending machine selections concerning life: take that trauma out with a single finger pointed, push a button and resurrect the dead, bring my father to the coral beach he loves, where he will be so elated to find himself alive that he won't even mind those instants where the shells are too sharp beneath our toes and slice us. He will say, *how wonderful to be sliced but alive.*

9.

Mom and I will love my father in silence if he can never speak again. As we love the wild turkeys who gather in her yard. I'm sleeping at her house when I hear the doctor call in the middle of the night. I find her sitting on the toilet, holding the phone. The news isn't good. His heart rate is high and he's having trouble breathing. He's been put on an oxygen mask. Mom looks unnaturally still. I try to make a joke about finding her on the toilet because that's my job in this family: to generate darkly humorous moments in the face of great pain. She's laughing hard now. I hope I can make my dad laugh at least one last time. Post-toilet-scene, I know I can't fall asleep, so I keep repeating in my mind, *please bring all the fairies to my father*. I picture vividly these fairies, envision them here with us too, so that my father, daughter sleeping next to me, mother in the other room, and I are just surrounded in this rainbow light emanating from my bloodshot eyeballs. Then I rotate my eyes and try to illuminate anyone else who's hurting anywhere. If there's anything this experience has reinforced, it's how raw life can be, and how we can all use some light shot out of a crying person's eyes sometimes, a speculative prayer.

10.

Defining life is tricky but so, too, are definitions of death. Because we say something died but that thing is still there. It doesn't poof into the stratosphere. So death becomes about what it was at one time, then what it is after the mystery. A kind of temporal before and after, even if that entity appears very similar in space. It's a corpse now and not a body, suddenly. But that's just linguistics. In "The Body" episode of *Buffy*, even our vampire slayer can't fight off death when it comes for her mother. She puzzles over an element that has baffled thinkers for generations: how can her mother just become a body? And why can't she just come back and be her mother, transform from dead to alive, turn from corpse back to person, in that same arbitrary snap that took her in the other direction, a barrier also shaped by language and science? By what linguistic or scientific set of definitions did her beloved mother, Joyce, become Corpse? And how can she correct this bizarre mistake? She wants a redo. She's drinking fruit punch when she comes upon the inconceivable: Joyce will never again have fruit punch, or any drink for that matter. Or eggs. And nobody can adequately explicate this to Buffy.

11.

After I shoot up the world with rainbow light, it hits me: *I'm going to go through this with my mother too someday.* The nightlight illuminates my daughter's sleeping face, and I think: *she's going to go through this one day.* And then as a kind of after-wave of horror, I think, *she's going to go through this with me. I am going to be the one dying,* gasping for air like a fish, looking at her with haunted eyes, like, *how is this possible and why can't you fix it?* She won't know why she can't fix it, but she will know to rub my feet, hold my hand, sing to me, because this is the most ingrained kind of human knowledge, linked neurologically to the way kids don't have to be told how to soothe a kitten.

12.

After almost losing him Saturday night, and just waiting for that call, we wake up Sunday morning, choke down eggs, then rush to the hospital, thinking we are going to say goodbye. We hold onto him too tightly, and he really opens his eyes and sees us after they take off the oxygen mask. He has these enormous green eyes that are, I don't know how else to put it, bursting with awe that he's able to view us, that we are there. The connection electrifies me. He'd accepted it was all over and this is his second coming. He keeps trying to say things, and it's so frustrating that we can't understand. We do figure out he's trying to say *hi* at one point, in a wheezy exhale. And when I say *hi* back, he's flabbergasted. Back and forth in amazement over and over. We are discovering language. Communion.

13.

At one point I say, *are you trying to say you love us*? And he nods so hard it looks like it hurts his delicate neck stem. Then I place my hands on either side of his face, stare into his eyes, telegraphing all the things I want to say, letting him send whatever he needs back. I've never had an interaction like this. I suspect I never will again. Finally, words are unnecessary. We are living beyond language. Something that perhaps only proximity to death can enable. Maybe death could be less frightening if we remember the people we are now won't ever experience it. This was why Lucretius called death a *black hole*. Because it's a place our philosophical minds as we currently know them can never venture. But how to take my live mind and go there? Isn't that the role of the artist? If I may be so bold as to refer to myself in such an insufferable way?

14.

Cicero lost a daughter to birthing complications and used philosophy to get through it. After studying ancient approaches to grief, he wrote the *Consolation*. It's a mythical document because it was lost to history but then reinvented in fragments in the Renaissance, at least pieces of which remain potentially inauthentic like all knowledge. It was supposedly later read by John Adams, who found it to be *remarkable for an ardent hope and confident belief of a future State,* by which he meant heaven, where Cicero—or at least the Cicero of the reinvented manuscript—believed his daughter to reside, which is at least part of what gave him such consolation.

15.

My father starts to look terrified suddenly. He has seen something none of us can. I will wonder my whole life what that was. I don't know why, but I lay one hand on his forehead, the other on his heart, over all the tubes, and say, *the fairies are here and they're filling you with rainbow light and you feel so good do you feel it*? And he looks calmer now and nods. Here's the thing: this whole experience is a black hole and yet I'm able to hug him for hours and hold his hand and tell him I'm holding his hand and he just keeps searching for me and then when he finds me right next to him I can watch him rediscover this unthinkable wonder. Which is simply that I'm right next to him. I promise this is not normally the kind of language I use but, together, right now, in this hospital room that smells like death, we are in a state of grace.

16.

His mental state is clearing up and he's trying to talk, even saying he's fine. The unthinkable: he's going to be aware of his body shutting down. I don't even know where to position my mind. All loss exists beyond language, but words are all I have for you. Or maybe it's really that existence was always beyond language, and we just didn't see it until faced with its ending. They have put some lip balm on him, and I'll always remember that aroma: a chemical rendition of berries plus something otherworldly. My mom and I talk incessantly, not wanting him to be in silence. She tells the story of how he almost drove his new sports car off a cliff in college and other excitements from when they were young. She's also trying to normalize things by boring him to tears with stories of the neighbors that include every last detail, as she normally does. After he wrote the *Consolation*, Cicero was assassinated. Did he end up in heaven, that future state? Who's to say? That question is what so much of this hinges on. *Who exactly is to say?* Nobody. And yet we still want to know. So how to proceed? In the first sentence of the book, Cicero writes, *I know the experts say not to treat recent traumas, and that in human life, no tragedy should strike us as surprising or unexpected. Still, though, I must try—if there's any possible way—to fix myself, and stop my world from caving in.* I write to you from a caved-in world. I'm still trying to dig my way out.

17.

Today is eclipse day. As I'm standing with my glasses on, squinting up at the obstructed sun, my mother calls to say the nurse will do morphine and it will all be over soon. Sitting on the Metro North train, crawling towards Southeast, to my dying father, leafless trees whipping by, thinking on endings, I'm reading Don DeLillo's *White Noise: It was these secondary levels of life, these extrasensory flashes and floating nuances of being, these pockets of rapport forming unexpectedly, that made me believe we were a magic act, adults and children together, sharing unaccountable things.* The lady sitting next to me asks where I'm headed. When I tell her, she pulls the cross necklace from her neck and places it around mine. I'm stunned, uncertain how to react, so I thank her. From the train, I call a local car service. It's always the same strange man who comes. I wonder if there are any other drivers and if he will murder me. He's that scary. When the car pulls up, there he is. As we rumble onward, I'm taking in the sights, seeing everything for my father since soon he won't be able to see any of it. Ways of seeing. The inevitable breakdown of all things. But also the reinvention, the reconfiguration. What will my father become? What will he see as he goes? What has he seen while he was here?

18.

Soon after my father was diagnosed with Multiple Myeloma, we went to see a movie together that asks just these sorts of existential questions, *Blade Runner 2049*, a sequel to Ridley Scott's 1982 original. It's just this sort of precariousness that *2049's* K faces, just as Rick Deckard did in the first one. As even a minor character from Philip K. Dick's 1968 source novel, *Do Androids Dream of Electric Sheep,* puts it, *Mors certa, vita incerta;* death is certain, life uncertain. Leaving the city is an exercise in unreality, the trees too bright, stage props, movie stuff. I merge with the seat leather, inhaling deeply car aroma and what passes for my own inner life in the twenty-first century. I pivot to take in scenery. Streaks of green tearing by as my silent driver speeds. No more buildings. We are crossing into a different land, foretold by the car's smoky scent of vanilla and death. The driver, who never speaks to me, must have had a cigar then tried to hide it with the lurching air freshener. Something we don't discuss enough is how little free will an air freshener has, how governed by vehicular determinism. The real issue we need to bring to our state assemblies is the dearth of air freshener agency and representation. I'm just fucking with you. The world has infinite real problems.

19.

But there's something to that smell. It summons lost, melancholic things, places I'll never see again, fragmented facts that visit me at certain times, like right now, as I trace the word *survive* into the window condensation, I remember how Mary Shelley's father taught her to write by following with her finger the letters of her dead mother's name on her grave. A cheery little thought. I give myself over to this darkness that surfaces, but I also feel it to be a presentiment of things to come. I have nothing to pull me back to cerebral stability since I'm about to lose half of what made me. Someone up there just suddenly said, *burn it all down*, and that was that. I pledge myself to this new nation of curving trees that speed by. They have no knowledge of my future loss, and I like it that way. I'm one with these window-scraping greens, the odor of annihilation inside. I imagine starting a new line of deathless people in this tree country before I pull myself together.

20.

Both *Blade Runner* films highlight this uncertain life with its inevitable questions: what makes us human, what makes us, and what will unmake us? In *2049* K is regularly tested for signs of this very questioning. In order to ensure he hasn't developed any dangerous signs of humanity, K's administered the Post-Trauma Baseline Test, phrases he must respond to, which are actually lines from the title poem of Nabokov's astounding novel, *Pale Fire*. After a near-death experience, John Shade perceives, *A system of cells interlinked within / Cells interlinked within cells interlinked / Within one stem. And dreadfully distinct / Against the dark, a tall white fountain played.* This vision becomes a metaphysical thread that Shade follows to further understand life and whatever lies beyond. The Post-Trauma Baseline Test gets trickier after K embarks on his journey toward a soul and all the angst this entails.

21.

At one point, windows wide open, the whole car fills with the smell of something dead. Maybe roadkill, something crushed beneath tires moving through regions never meant to be paved, the land's way of rebelling, speaking back in a language only I can decipher. One way or another, the stench seems to be a form of communication. But I'm unable to interpret it. I have a sense I should pay more attention. I wonder often about the world's cruel inventions. I sense we're headed towards a reckoning but I'm here for it. There are disasters-in-the-making from which we dare not look away. I am, in short, a rubbernecker, even when it's my own accident. In *Do Androids Dream of Electric Sheep*, the characters address these existential growing pains in much the same manner as we do today. In the face of an unthinkable existence, they pray or watch television. Deckard lives in a world of perpetual TV and mood organs that allow him to control his emotions. Authenticity, even authentic pain, is hard to come by.

22.

The driver zooms on, and a bird suddenly flies into the windshield, an explosion of feathers and blood. I'm heartbroken about the bird, about my dad, about a world in which both are possible. I wonder if it was a parent bird with kids who will mourn it. Was it a father bird? A mother bird? Just then my phone rings and it's my own mom as though, as always, she has sensed from miles away that I was thinking about her, or just generally having mother-related thoughts at all. *Are you coming now?* she asks, her voice no longer her own. I tell her I'll be there soon, that I love her. She puts the phone up to his ear so I can tell him I love him too. I wonder what it all sounds like to him right now? The ocean?

23.

In one memorable scene in *2049*, K's virtual girlfriend Joi employs an emanator to attain a physical body. She feels the raindrops falling on her skin in a sequence that reminds us how a simple moment such as this can be holy somehow, when we come up against the shock of being alive. But then Joi pauses, frozen in mid-ecstasy when K receives a voicemail. Of course, the real question androids raise is not whether they are truly human but whether we are. Joi's freezing makes us ponder our own times when technological disturbances from the outside world can invade our most private moments. We recognize this future and its onslaught of increasingly invasive technologies that fracture human closeness as our present, which is only fitting since the first *Blade Runner* was set around now.

24.

I soon become distracted by the easy beauty of my surroundings, twisting groves of trees where you could lose your mind. Pines lining the mountains like—who was it that said it again?—*tongues of flame*. I hallucinate a new life for myself out here, an arboreal existence where I have trees for limbs and live among the forest creatures. I would be their queen. Maybe I'll stay here and never face the hospital, leaving reality altogether at last. As it gets later, the trees throw shadows, and we enter the kind of quiet you only get in the countryside. The effect hurls me, unwilling, into thoughts of the past, both the recent and long-gone. The shaped darkness continues to work its elegiac spell, and I am forced to remember what I'm speeding towards.

25.

As you might have guessed by now, the frightening realization that eventually dawns on us is that the androids are us. I'm fairly certain that more than a few people today would fail the book's Voight-Kampff Empathy Test designed to tell human from machine. It's not merely that androids aren't human enough but that humans aren't either. As we continue, something lights up my periphery, and there appear to be several small fires blazing along the woods. The driver pulls the car over and jumps out. Suddenly, I'm so tired my eyes are starting to close, and I must fight them open. It could be the act of quickly opening, then closing, the world becoming something glimpsed only now and then, or some trick of light, but for an instant I think I see the fire through the driver's body, as though he's suddenly transparent. He has brought a jug of water from the car, and he pours it over the fires that I can see before heading deeper into the woods.

26.

It's probably all the creepy things that have happened since I got into this car, but I start to feel like something sinister is in there with me. The driver doesn't come back for a while. I weigh the dangers within and without and decide to get out of the car. I don't want to die out there, but I don't want to die in here either. Not before I get to say goodbye to my father. As I push further into the woods, there the driver is, digging in the dirt like a dog. For a moment it looks like his face is covered in blood. But when I look again, it's gone. My eyes are gaining a mind of their own. Clouds cover the moon, throwing us into a darkness that feels like beginning times, before late capitalism and the colonization of this earth. It would be lovely if I weren't scared to death.

27.

As we get back into the car, there's a chorus of howling from outside. I turn to look out the window, wondering if I can shrink myself and escape through the tiny crack at the top. If we weren't driving so fast, I might open the door and roll out onto the road, taking my chances with the coyotes and lone wolf. If only to put off discovering the truth about my father's fate. But I can't risk missing saying goodbye to him. The driver turns back to look at me, eyes now wild, rolls his window all the way down, throws his head back, and executes a howl that almost takes my ears off. A long dark sound like I've never heard. A sound to stop time. To stop all ideas about time. It seems to stretch from all angles, carrying the suffering of variegated creatures, but it also feels strangely close-up, like maybe it's coming from me, capturing all I've been through, but also gesturing towards where I might travel if I'd only blow open my brain paths, as this sound was probably in the process of doing for me, whether I liked it or not. It's deathly but, I have to admit, also seductive, a siren song I must close my ears against lest I lose everything. But before I know it, I'm rolling down my window, howling out into the great beyond. The driver looks delighted, taking his own bellows up an octave in salute.

28.

The denizens of Dick's book eventually conclude that their religion, Mercerism, and even empathy itself, is a *swindle*. So much of what we accept daily is a horror, from the knowledge of what we do to other creatures to our own deaths hovering somewhere before us. As Nabokov's poet Shade frames it, *A syllogism: other men die; but I /Am not another; therefore I'll not die. / Space is a swarming in the eyes; and time / A singing in the ears. In this hive I'm / Locked up.* And so what's left? The whole car journey hovers outside experience. It all would have been too much for me at one time in my life. But with my current mindset, I accept it. In fact, I suspect it can be no other way. I tell myself it's just like a weird trip, complete with all those odd highs and lows. Except real. The only thing left to do is to let go. I learned this from my father, a most mystical man.

29.

Instantly, I'm a student of terror, understanding its full contours, but also something I'd never seen before: it can also be a way of seeing, a mode of doing away with all that came before, a visual clearing. I have the urge to grab up a stick from the ground and write all this down but we're still driving. I've always been a timid writer. That's the problem. Until now. Something in me has shifted. I want to tell others about my newfound wisdom, my metaphysics of terror, a neo-vision that I'm sure would work even with my eyes closed. Nothing can close this aperture once opened. And I want it to stay this way. Perhaps there is nowhere to go from here except back to Shade from *Pale Fire*, who finds that, *This / Was the real point, the contrapuntal theme;/ Just this: not text, but texture; not the dream / But topsy-turvical coincidence.* And so, like a good android, I cling to my own implanted memories, my own glittering delusion of humanity, the rain falling on my emanated hands, *not text but texture.* We arrive. I enter the hospital.

30.

There's a man walking with his wife around the atrium in his hospital socks. I think on how hard a time he's having, how empty his wife's eyes are, how she looks uncaring. But I've sat by my father's hospital beds enough to know the look is in fact one of caring too much, so much that there's no caring left at the moment, nothing but the memory of caring, still a place of deepest love, but the content has fallen to the bottom, and when you try to find it there are just echoes. If you go home and shower and get a change of clothes, you can find it again. Things fall apart is what I can see. But how to put them back together? Or maybe that's too human a way of thinking of it. Maybe putting things back together is not the aim. Maybe this is what death is trying to teach me.

31.

As I walk by room after room of heartbroken people crying over some suffering being, only here briefly, whom they are realizing they're losing forever, I choke on something I can only describe as the holy. Because it is only when you stare into the maw of total ugliness that you start to see complete beauty, that they are the same thing, that if you go far enough around one you come to the other. You can rehearse for this moment through speculative fiction, but it will still not have the zing of the actual: the smell of Papa's hospital room when I walk in is that of dying, even if only my animal self knows it.

32.

At one point a priest comes to give the last rites and it feels cinematic—a film I wouldn't normally be appearing in or watching. He's a Catholic of course, but he also says he can do Jewish or even atheist prayers, which is why we let him in. Do we want it? Yes, very much. And so, with Jeanne and the nurse named Audrey—who wears Hoka sneakers, and initially seemed cold, but whom we love now because she found my father the socks he likes—we all place our hands upon my father and listen as the priest prays over him. I do feel somewhat healed just by being in the room with this man who regularly travels through spaces of death and lives to tell of it. As the priest finishes up, I feel something inside me glow that has to do with pain, but also with a kind of opening of my skin to let the entirety of the world in, with all its moods, not just the parts I choose or can handle, unedited, unexpurgated, true. A state of the sublime.

33.

Trouble is that my father is not healed. He is now struggling for breath, and something has changed in him. He looks like he has given up. There's a flash I will never unsee in the eyes of this man who has been like my own skin, who knows he's about to die. This must be the saddest sight of all. We sing to him, we hold him, we tell him every story we can remember, but he just looks resigned. They have turned everything off. It is just a matter of holding him and waiting now. I try to tell a joke because I know no other way. He attempts to raise that one corner of his mouth but it's too much for him now that he's on the way out. Mom plays Parsifal and I read him his favorite poem, Cavafy's "Ithaka." They turn his vital signs monitor fuchsia to indicate that they are no longer trying to keep him alive, and they give him a fuchsia armband. My mom and I both want to take the armband home to be closer to him but don't ask. We only find this out when we compare notes afterward. The nurses close the curtain and give us time to be alone with him.

34.

This is my most vivid recollection of him: riding those waves and seeking coral, an already dead material by the time it washes up all white on shore, sea bones, at Soldier Point in Culebra, off the coast of Puerto Rico, where my father has asked for his ashes to be scattered, nodding vigorously in the hospital when we asked if he wanted to go back there. It was only afterward that I realized he might have meant he was ready to go home: that, yes, he wanted to visit Culebra again, which means snake in Spanish, but not alive, dead.

35.

My mother and I wrap our arms too tightly around him and cover him with kisses. I'm sobbing and I realize rubbing snot all over his face, but I think he forgives me. We are saying *I love you love you love you,* like an incantation to bring him back. I call him *papa,* which I haven't done since childhood. There's a splinter of time, which we find impossible to identify, where we are holding my living father, and then we are holding my dead father. It stops thought. It stops time. It stops.

36.

I scream out, a child again suddenly, *papa, don't leave me.* My mother comes behind and holds me. I tell her I don't understand. She tells me nobody does. We hug harder than we ever have, and I clear a tendril of wet hair from her eye. We sit for a long time holding his hand. Until the man from the funeral home comes to take him. I know he's only trying to help but I fight back an urge to strike him as he takes my father from me. As we are hobbling out of the room, I look back to see the empty bed where my father was, the lone Birthday King balloon hovering over it.

37.

Later, my mom asks the funeral home guy if he died in Danbury or Carmel. The guy says, *well if he died in Danbury, then he died in Danbury, and if he died in Carmel he died in Carmel.* Famous last words. The man seems not to get that my mother has just lost her person and is out of her mind with grief. There are things nobody tells you: like you must arrange for your loved one's body to be picked up from the hospital. It all feels like giving birth in that you are undergoing this horrifying miracle and there's still paperwork and so much nobody told you about. And no one will ever entirely understand what you went through, even if they've gone through it themselves.

38.

Afterward, they ask if we want an autopsy, and my mom and I almost laugh, saying how my father would have found this hilarious— after we have watched this disease waste him for the past years and there's little mystery as to the culprit. It's too bad my dad missed that one. I add it to the list of things to tell him if I ever see him again. My father is gone. My mind breaks. So I look to Yoda: *Death is a natural part of life. Rejoice for those around you who transform into the Force. Mourn them do not. Miss them do not. Attachment leads to jealousy. The shadow of greed, that is.* I now have a different view on the world. I see how it ends and it's not pretty, but it is transformative. This realization that we are all just these spirits floating around, that we all end in the same way, and how every instant we get is a shattering miracle. I don't see how I can think the same way I did before all this happened, and I don't think I want to.

III.

DEATH AS *FURIOSA*

1.

In the weeks after my father dies, we attempt normality, but my life spins off into speculative fiction. Going to see *Furiosa* alone in the theater soon after losing him, and with the world on fire, is shattering. I feel the rumble of this woman warrior inside me until I think maybe the movie theater's exploding. I wonder often how I'll handle this city if it becomes a war zone, of my role as writer-cook and History Woman—in the terms of the *Mad Max* universe—in post-apocalyptic Brooklyn. Since my daughter is sad to start school again after the loss, I tell her that it's looking for magic in the day that creates it. I hope for all our sake's this is true. These are the sorts of lies we often tell as parents, ones we hope to make true. Or maybe that's the ultimate speculative fiction.

2.

There are stories where the protagonist is a cartographer of her own destiny, but my life has always been more picaresque. *What would happen if one woman told the truth about her life? Would the world explode?* I text my clever friend Emily. I reach out of bed at her ding. She has texted back: *trouble is nothing would effing change if she did.* But what if it did? What would that even look like? I pivot: decide to look at those stark truths but through the lens of speculative fiction. It's by way of the fabrications, the coming at it all from outlandish angles, unthinkable perspectives that we can really see how things are here on earth, and how they need to change. I move through so many virtual worlds each day it's starting to turn my mind into a frazzled, networked ooze, so I need some sort of lens to understand this life, this death.

3.

So many theories of death are laced with the enchanted belief that it's something we can outthink. Or that with all these fancy words and notions about meaning-making and love, I could ever possibly forget how sad my father looked in his last moments when he realized he was about to die. That is something I can never un-see. Or the guilt I feel at being alive when the one who made me is not, like I'm some evil Pinocchio. Come back, Geppetto, I'm not a real boy yet. But Geppetto is silent. I envision him hovering over me, hugging me as I cry. What else can I imagine? His body in an incinerator, his ashes in my mother's garden, some to Culebra? The ring he always wore in a box by my computer. I'm wearing it right now as I write, some more of his ashes in a box covered with angels on top of my bookshelf. I know he feels at home with my books and my angels. Come back, Geppetto. I'm so alone and still made of wood. The pain has seeped through my wooden chest and it's splintering me. No wonder we love happy endings. They make us believe however briefly that we will be the one to cheat death.

4.

A weather update pings in. A flood is coming. I check if everything's been canceled. None of it has. My son's telling me about the Inca project he will be presenting later when I come to his school this morning. I will shuttle between his classroom and his sister's. They will both never feel they had enough time with me. I will be exhausted as always, halved, in need of a double. *When in danger the sea-cucumber divides itself in two: / one self it surrenders for devouring by the world, / with the second it makes good its escape,* writes Wisława Szymborska in "Autotomy." Also, I will feel entirely invested in the Inca peoples. If my memory of middle school history serves me, the conquistadors arrived to find the Incas weakened by civil war and various epidemics, much like what's happening now.

5.

Violence permeates everything. Yesterday, right in front of my door, with my children sleeping inside, cops tried to break this man's windows with batons, as the car backed as hard as it could into the cars in front, behind. There's a Virgin Mary statue in front of the church on the corner, who watched as he then drove on the sidewalk until he could turn into oncoming traffic, the cops in pursuit. I watched, too, but I'm not a virgin, which is why the kids were asleep in my home at the time instead of never having been born, it could be said. The History Man narrates *Furiosa*. The books were burned after the fall, and these history men tattooed the past onto their skin to remember. He is the poet and storyteller, the only one Dementus keeps around who's not a warrior. He wants to teach Furiosa his ways so that she may become indispensable.

6.

The History Man does end up leaving Dementus in the end. When he sees Furiosa heading off in her vehicle made of discarded parts that she has reconfigured, he calls her, *The Darkest of Angels, The Fifth Rider of the Apocalypse*. I hallucinate myself as Furiosa—even Dementus, if only to drive a chariot of motorcycles through the Wasteland—but I know I'll more likely be one of the war boys. Ideally, Guitar Guy, who plays the flame-throwing electric guitar, vibrating on the front of the tank. In director George Miller's interpretation of the story, Guitar Guy sought out work in the mines because he was born blind, taking his guitar with him underground until Immortan Joe's henchmen heard his music and made him a bad guy. The actor who plays Guitar Guy created his own Texas Chainsaw-worthy backstory for his character, viewing him as having been seized by Immortan Joe's men while holding onto his mother's decapitated head, and then using her face to make the mask he wears, a gory tribute.

7.

But I'm none of those characters. Back in this reality, I sit on the toilet while my daughter attempts to braid my bangs, the whole bathroom shaking not with battle but with the forever construction that's been taking place on my Brooklyn block since we moved in five years ago. I imagine they're constructing a secret other city beneath this one, and I will be its first citizen if my son fires one more videogame shotgun while living in that second body. In Fortnite they call it a skin. I figure they're building this other city as a kind of do-over, and this one will be less violent. My daughter's telling me what's most important to her right now concerning her future, and it's that she's not required to join the army because she doesn't want to wear a ponytail. I laugh loudly when she says this, but I'm also forced to see how she has armies on the mind, during Israel-Palestine, Ukraine-Russia and the current civil war in our country that even a Hollywood movie now must acknowledge.

8.

What I like about death in movies is that the dead people are played by actors. They get up afterwards, joke around, get something to eat, maybe even do another take, dying over and over. Death in *Furiosa* involves a flame-throwing electric-guitar player. Death in real life is not as fun. There's no getting up after. That we know of. After my father dies, I go to the movies a lot to escape into virtual worlds, at least partly because I'm hoping to catch a glimpse of him onscreen, feel comforted that he's found an entertaining virtual world to inhabit, one where I can come and see him any time, maybe even share some popcorn through the screen, extra butter always.

9.

When I go to the movies, some other universe opens inside me and I'm everyone at once. My heart beats so fast I'm afraid it will have an attack. I want to grab everyone in the theater and yell, spittle-close to their faces, just raining down on them, *isn't this such a spectacle? How could anyone ever think this is just normal*? While the movie plays, I am lost in the darkness and motion of light, the sonics, such that I leave Brooklyn, literally enter the movie world. One time they couldn't find me afterwards for weeks. They combed the screen but only came away with sticky pink stuff on their hands that my son later identified as me by the smell alone—Aqua di Gio and desperation.

10.

I often compose my writing in my head at the theater, and sometimes I use the little light they have under the tables at Nitehawk to scribble in my notebook. I'm not enough of a jerk to take out my phone during the movie and write in my Notes app. I do have some boundaries. It's not just the movie theater that does this to me. I feel over-excited pretty much all the time. I want to grab people, even during faculty meetings, and holler about how we'll all die someday, but we're alive right now in the same room, and isn't that bloody unbelievable? Since my father has passed, I also want to ask them what they think will happen to their bodies after a nurse puts the fuchsia bracelet on them, turns their screen fuchsia? I truly want to know, but I do have some social grace, so I don't ask. Instead, I inquire if they're taking the F or G train home and make a joke about running for the G every time like it's some sort of social experiment. As usual, I halve myself to live. I consider it a real friend when I can just throw my guts against the wall, and they don't flinch, they're like, *I can read that.*

11.

The ground feels so shifting underneath me. In the faculty meeting yesterday, we discovered that yes there is cause for celebration in that there *may* be a Fall semester. Yesterday, after class, in the middle of speaking to a student about how she shouldn't worry about anything, an alarm and flashing lights came on, and an announcement said to please ignore the smell in the hallways, that they were investigating a sulfur leak. With the whole sulfur thing, I had the irrational thought, before directing students towards the staircases, that the devil had finally arrived, and it explained so much lately. I also wondered if it had any intel on the hereafter.

12.

I also don't ask the people at the faculty meeting if sometimes reading the news and thinking too closely about the state of things almost breaks them, makes them imagine their communities as post-apocalyptic *Mad Max* wastelands. George Miller was torn between calling it *Mad Max: Fury Road* and *Mad Max: Furiosa*. At first Furiosa was going to refer to the land around Fury Road, so she had from the beginning geographical proportions, her veins the roots of the story always. My daughter, too, is of geographical proportions (I'm entirely unbiased, speaking as her mother of course). I've recently cut her thicket of curls, which used to almost graze her waist, into a bob. She holds back the whole hedge maze with the sparkly rainbow headband I got her. As I brush it for her, I find the paint I always find, even though I force showers on them at seven-thirty every night, because she's always making something. Last night at my mom's house, she disappeared for a while, and we came to the field to find a whole sculptural stick village. She'd made a special little hut where her dead grandfather could read his heavy books even if, as she put it, *he's only in the clouds now.*

13.

I stand in front of the mirror to put my contacts in, trying to do normal things to avoid losing my mind in a world that has, like the Fortnite game blaring outside the battalion of my bathroom door, decidedly jumped the shark. My daughter gets on her step stool beside me, our two faces different paths one face could take. She's lifting her lid, too, because I am. I get confused for a second and think I'm looking at my younger self in the mirror, another form of time travel. Before lifting my other lid, I bury my face in what remains of her curls, knowing I will find more paint there; I'd be disappointed if I didn't. When I do this, my shoulders drop temporarily from their raised state of bracing for the next shock, where they always seem to be lately. I even wake from sleep to find my back sore, right where the wings would be, as though I secretly fly around all night, only to land back in my bed. What a waste of a magical nocturnal skill. What I really hope I'm doing with all this flying around is being heroic in some way, protecting the hurting citizens of the world with…what skills exactly? I'll have to think about that. What's worthwhile for people anymore? This: my head in my daughter's hair.

14.

Yet, as I brush my teeth, she tells me all about her Lenape diorama project I will see when I go to the school later and, since I'm a History Woman of the *Mad Max* universe, I wonder if the children know what really happened to the Lenape people so that they could have this life here in Brooklyn. How to tell them the real stories that hover behind their cheerfully constructed world? I try, and she nods at me wisely, like she has known all along that the Disney castles were secretly upheld by the forced labor of dolphins. She's what they used to call an old soul. Later, she will take me on a tour of her diorama, pointing at the cardboard Lenape people, and noting that they are all dead now *because colonialization.*

15.

My daughter's diorama is yet another virtual world I've passed through today, but so is this typing. Writing has always been a way of coping with difficult realities and even trying to transform them. Tomi Adeyemi wrote *Children of Blood and Bone* as a way of dealing with the unexperienceable experience of turning on the news and hearing that another unarmed black person had been killed by the police. She knew she couldn't solve the complex problem with one book, but she thought reaching even one reader was something. Some say it's escapist to deal with these real-world issues in fantasy lands, but this coming at it slant is how people can hear it. At any rate, telling people directly is not working.

16.

Five minutes later, more virtual words spring up and our apartment is a war zone. Minecraft now blaring from my son's room as my daughter's *Magic School Bus* audiobook reveals Mrs. Frizzle and the kids to be lost in space. My daughter and I do our morning routine where we sit, holding handfuls of birdseed out the window. Because a bird once sat in my hand when I did that, and now my daughter thinks I'm an avian-whispering sorceress. I don't correct her because who else will ever think this about me? Since my mom left the city, her life is just one long unlikely-animal-friends video, and I'm jealous over here as we watch angry city pigeons fight over an ancient piece of bagel. But today we sit with hands outstretched and a bird does in fact come. It's a pigeon, but still. Its claws grasping onto my hand feel like esoteric messages. My daughter looks at me like I've conjured the pigeon. Again, I don't correct this. Her eyes are enormous as she tries to put her hand underneath mine to take over, but does so too quickly, and the bird flies away. But her gesture causes our birdless hands to be holding.

17.

When she was little, she always wanted to be in a carrier, which means I wore her like a baby kangaroo every minute I was awake. Our body heat, one person's doubled, was unimaginable. This was heightened when I wore her while cooking, accidentally dribbling olive oil on her head as I bit into the garlic bread to test it. She would look up at me, as I showered her with food driblets, with a knowing expression, like, *of course you've done this again, it's so you.* Then she would make this obscene squirrel-eating-a-nut motion with her mouth and tiny hands, ghost-consuming along with me the solid food she didn't yet have the hardware to manage, until I ugly-laughed so hard I would have dropped her if she weren't in a carrier. I see now that this was an act of imagination on her part. My relationship with my daughter remains pretty much the same now that she's seven. She always wants to be up against my body. I wish I could wear her in a carrier, but it would have very different implications now. I still dribble foodstuffs on her regularly. Then she gives me that look. I don't ever want to let her go. I will. But I don't want to. I am greedy for her. I didn't want to let my father go. I don't want to let my own life go. But I must let her go, let her grow up. I must let my father go. I must let myself go. I must one day die. I must start doing it now so I'm ready when the time comes. But I also must live. That takes a mechanism of letting go as well. Again, the poetics of poaching an egg.

18.

First, I see *Furiosa*, and then when I rewatch *Fury Road* I become hypnotized by the idioms of speculative fiction and action movies. With the expansiveness of imagined worlds, I can feel my mind growing larger to fit both the intense joy and suffering of these imagined communities. When I leave the theater after *Furiosa*—a transition from imaginary to real I always find painful on a bodily level—and get back on the subway, I start to perceive the world as a similarly cutthroat, choreographed disaster movie as I duck and cover through the potentially violent, always absurd action sequence that is my life here in the city. When I get home, I start reading up on classical histories to try to understand this absolute war zone I'm entering—battles all over the world, rising fascism, climate issues, subway bomb threats, my kids' public school locking down due to warnings of violence, Covid still, floods, wildfires, misinformation, violence in politics, politics in violence. Yes, all the joy but also the hellscapes I'd already been through in the past and survived, and now losing my father.

19.

The biggest change to my aging face—I notice as I look at it side-by-side with my daughter's in the mirror—is a set of subtle new creases over my eyelids, like a mirror-set of lids, or like my eyes are trying to create hoods so they don't have to witness the destruction of father or world, or father-world. I bring the kids to school and attend Drop Everything and Read Time. It's flooding out there. Because of the amount of water, we practically have to swim there. Meanwhile, books are being banned all over the United States, so this feels necessary. I may need to become a History Woman sooner than I thought. We take the kids to our local library branch every Sunday like it's church. Afterwards, I again almost swim to teach. As I'm leaving class, I post a picture, to what was once known as Twitter, of cars practically floating in the street water and write: *Tell me now that climate issues are in our imaginations here in Brooklyn.* I know I'm being somewhat provocative, but I can't foresee how fast it will spread, and how much rage it will uncork in the American psyche. It begins picking up likes, views, and retweets with astounding velocity. At first, it's a mixture of those for and against the concept of climate change but then things take a turn.

20.

What is our source of radical hope? In the *Mad Max* universe, it's called The Green Place or The Place of Abundance, inhabited by the matriarchal Vuvalini of Many Mothers, including Furiosa and her mother, Mary Jabassa. Are we heading towards the souring of the Green Place? Has it already happened? Is this the Wasteland? But you know what happened to it in *Fury Road* when Furiosa tried to take the Five Wives there? It had become the creepy crow place. The crow people are the Vulvani who stayed—stilt-walking sky fishers adorned in crow feathers who use the stilts to stay above the poisonous bog. It's a heart-stopping sight. Logic-stopping sight. I am the Vulvani who stayed. I am getting my stilts and crow feathers ready.

21.

Early in the life of the tweet, one person poses a question that seems valid about whether this isn't also a matter of draining and infrastructure, and I acknowledge that, yes, it's also that, and it infuriates them. Others make the only-to-some-extent valid point that this was flooding, not climate change, and they link to images of historical flooding in New York City. Which, yes, okay, but, as still others point out, it isn't that there has never been flooding before, but rather it's the incredible increase in these events that's concerning, indicative of, yes, climate changes. But it seems it's my trying to see various points that most enrages them. Not even the claim of climate change but the possibility of things being not merely polar. At one point, Dementus captures Furiosa and Praetorian Jack. He chains Furiosa by her arm and forces her to watch as he drags Jack to his death behind a motorcycle. But she rips her arm off (some say gnaws it off—there are different takes in various virtual communities), later fashioning a new arm from found items that's a thing of beauty, and for me serves as a symbol of creativity in the face of terrible trauma.

22.

Back in the real world, my climate change tweet becomes a war ground for the polarized viewpoints that have brought us into an undeclared, but everyone knows about it, kind of Civil War here in the United States. There are people who attempt to employ research, and I have respect for that, but they are overcome by the many who say things essentially like, *this flood was to drown the sinning immigrants of the city* sort of thing or *god's will for NYC and its LGBTQ freaks.* There are also those who quote the tweet, along with my profile picture, and attempt to discern my heritage, with comments made about my possible immigrant status, how I should have been kept out of the US by force, or even been impaled on a fence while trying to invade it. The posts employ a stunning array of words designed to communicate with linguistic precision, language as scalpel, what should happen to me because of this tweet.

23.

There are also of course those who suggest various things I can do with the tweet, what bodily orifices I can insert it in—with useful anatomically diagrammatic language, thank you very much, to explain the exact geography of what I can do with the tweet on my bodily surface, mapped to the last mile of my potentially immigrant flesh—and how it would really help everyone if I would delete the tweet, my account or, better yet, just die already, and/or kill myself in a menu of entertaining ways. Many men offer, very dapperly, to rape me, some are even kind enough to throw in a ritualized killing at the end. They are all so very kind. Selfless even. (If you don't understand why I'm joking about this, please see Chantal V. Johnson in *Post-Traumatic* on *the humor of traumatized people, a humor that made most people so uncomfortable*.) This is not the first time I have been threatened with these outcomes. It all started in childhood as it does for many. At least this time they don't seem to be carried out.

24.

When Furiosa comes upon Dementus, he says she looks like something that has come back from hell, that the only thing powerful enough to do that is hate, not hope. He sees hate as one of the great engines. She asks if he has any recollection of what he did to her mother—a sort of crucifixion—and how he made her watch, saying she wants both her lost childhood and her mother back. He tells her he has lost his family too and nothing will ever make it better. No amount of revenge. He tells her to shoot him from behind. He collapses. When he awakens, now he recognizes his history with her. He says he was waiting for a successor, a new him. She says no, but he says she's already dead. The question is: can she make it epic now? Temporalities and story specifics are not meant to be exact since George Miller sees the *Mad Max* universe as the sort of folklore passed around after dark in the Wasteland, a kind of historiography.

25.

We hear the History Man now at the end of *Furiosa*. He conveys the various iterations of the story in terms of what Furiosa might have done to Dementus: that she merely shot him; that she had done to him what he'd done to her mother, or what he'd done to Praetorian Jack; but she had told him herself—that emphasis on testimony—that she'd planted the peach pit her mother had given her right into his body, making of him a tree in the Citadel's hydroponic garden. Talk about turning the story around. Before I can muse anymore on the social media threats I'm receiving, I must rush to an eye appointment. An optometrist-in-training will be the one teaching me new ways of seeing. I slide my head to rest against the metal clamp, my chin in a sort of stirrup, my eyes attempting to focus on a little red barn. I want to go there. I imagine things would be simpler. I'm sure there is golden hay, that this is where the cattle of the sun are lowing. In addition to recommending wearing blue mascara while writing, Helen Oyeyemi says part of what inspires her speculative writing is the sense that time doesn't move how we suspect it does, and we don't talk about it enough. She likes to take the things of the world out of their usual mental home and fragment/reinvent them.

26.

My father is dead. It truly hits me, here at the eye doctor of all places. The fake red barn looks so peaceful, so small and so red. It's situated atop green grass. I want to go there so badly. I can feel the plant life responding to my toes. I imagine the world I might find there, so far from this city with its underground labyrinths and bloodshed. While the optometrist-in-training works, this Chevy commercial plays on repeat on a mounted television. In it the daughter calls her offscreen, and thus invisible, parents to tell them that because she bought this car her whole life is now falling into place. She can see it. And I just want to tell her about chaos, how all those pieces are going to fall apart time and again, and she will rebuild them, and make incredible creative structures, but how her quaint idea of things falling into place is just so hilarious right now as my father is dead.

27.

This Chevy girl will one day receive a call from one of those parents telling her the other is gone. How together will things feel then? But I have to say, though she isn't real, I don't wish this future on her for a second. The Chevy girl and her parents are imaginary, at least in terms of this world. The actress exists, yes, but not the character she is playing, so this daughter and these parents are deathless, sacred. I now appreciate the commercial more. It is all we have of heaven. In the eye exam, they test the pressure, and I wonder if all that's been going on will influence the outcome. I imagine the various parts of my life as real cows of oversized proportions, who have escaped the fake barn from the eye test, and are running wild, just stampeding all over my face. They're magnificent, though, these charging, enormous cattle. They're worth it. Or so I tell myself. When he says the pressure is normal, I choke back dark laughter. He gives me a brief, questioning look, and I try to telepath to him that he's better not knowing. He nods his head like he gets it. And perhaps he does. The optometrist wouldn't get it, but the optometrist-in-training understands life's constant state of contingency. This is why I like him.

28.

Now that I've found this conceptual space, growing larger by the day, between the things of the world and me, it just keeps enlarging, especially as death pervades, surrounds me, reminding me of our ultimate inevitable demise. Things are getting further away, all the buzzing noise replaced with something silent inside me. Maybe one of the biggest differences I notice since my dad departed is this noiseless calm. I am still jabbering and teaching and giving readings but there is a kind of interior hush now. Maybe I'm making a space for my father to live. My mom keeps reminding me how, when he was diagnosed with Cancer, my atheist dad started saying *thy will be done* in response to any uncertain situation, which of course is all of them. This reminds me of the Tralfamadorians saying *so it goes* in Kurt Vonnegut's *Slaughterhouse Five*.

29.

Vonnegut invents Tralfamadore and the time-traveling lead Billy Pilgrim, so we get trauma as time-crisis, drawing on Vonnegut's experience of being a German prisoner of war during the Dresden bombing. In the book Billy becomes an optometrist after marrying Valencia. (I imagine Billy as the gentleman currently rooting around in my eyeballs.) They have two kids, and on the day of his daughter's wedding, Billy's abducted by the Tralfamadorians, who can see four dimensionally—all elements of space-time simultaneously, creating a plane where death is meaningless and met with *so it goes*. When a Tralfamadorian dies, it only looks that way because they are still living in the past, although they apparently still have funerals. Which is all to say: obviously I'm hoping my dad is a Tralfamadorian.

30.

Vonnegut says his books are *mosaics made up of a whole bunch of tiny little chips; and each chip is a joke.* But there's something very serious here, too: Vonnegut was there as war prisoner. This fragmented, time-traveling narrative processes traumatic memory. The mind can't grasp unspeakable things in the present, and when you look back on it, try to write about it, it can become even more unreachable and science-fictional-seeming, we as eccentric, fractured pained characters moving through various times and spaces, all at once in ways that don't make sense to anyone else, much less to ourselves. So he becomes a student of his own experience, disowned onto Billy who is, after all, a pilgrim. Just as I try to become a student of time, space, creativity and sorrow, but also something transcendent, something about the beyond here.

31.

What distinguishes this beyond, at least partially, is its unthinkability. It lives past thought, so how to think my way there? Maybe the key is to stop thinking altogether and do something more futuristic. Tralfamadore does away with the linear, and allows you to look at all moments at once, to inspect any given one, in much the same way Joan Didion describes in her memoir of the trauma of her husband's death and her daughter's hospitalizations, when she wishes for a digital means to allow her to change how time and space works, to be able to show the reader all the memories, and let us choose from various readings of them. She needs something greater, more capacious than language, time, space as they stand.

32.

When my mom accidentally emails me the dream society's obituary for my father from his own email account, and I see his little Gmail photo pop up—with its weird coloring that made him look like a ghost contacting me even when he was alive—I'm like, *I knew it.* I legitimately think he's emailing me to say, *it's all been a grave misunderstanding; it's actually a funny story.* It feels like I'm just missing something obvious. This is the last email that actual live Dad sent me on February eighteenth before all this happened: *Reading A Wrinkle in Time for what it has to say about the dark side, but also space and time. Please read it. It has a crucial message for you.* After I read this, I become a detective. It's bizarre how tears can hurt your eyes when they come from your eyes as though they're foreign bodies. Trouble is, I'm not Meg from *A Wrinkle in Time* and I can't take a tesseract through the folds of space-time to get my father back.

33.

Despite my historical, unpopular dislike of both meditation and yoga, after Papa passes, I start listening to this meditation app, created by a news anchor who had an on-air breakdown. When the meditation is really working for me—when I'm not fielding screaming children at the same time or surreptitiously checking my email—I have come to this place that exists, that has always been there presumably, beneath my eyelids. It's this whole new piece of real estate to me, though, a landscape of shelter and peace under all the chaos. I try to remember to go there frequently but in truth I often forget. What I spend a lot of time doing is checking under my eyelids in case my father is hiding there, hustling people at pool or something.

34.

Then, on the train on the way here to visit my mom, I close my eyes, and the sun plays over my eyelids, through the train window, causing this riot of imagery, intensive red and orange shapes just madly flashing in this same meditative landscape, this inner movie theater, and it's exquisite. I open my eyes, see the other people on the train, and get what I believe might be called a brief flash of enlightenment —forgive me for that phrasing; yes, I can hear myself—where I'm like: *I love all these people crumpling newspapers and drinking from water bottles. We are all linked, made from the same stuff as stardust. My dad died, dispersed into all that nature that I can see outside the train windows. One day I will die, and all my particles will also fly out into all that—same with everyone on this train. So there aren't as many distinctions as I once thought. Everything is permeable.*

35.

Bertrand Russell said the way to stop fearing death is to gradually open to the world, leaving behind the ego, and stretching until you are ready to merge with the wider world in the end, to put it entirely in my own words and perhaps incorrectly. I stare until I start to see those dots that I can only imagine as the fairies start moving in front of my eyes. I watch them, wondering if you can watch something eye-generated with those same eyes, and then I think on how we see things upside-down. A place beyond words. This is the kingdom we've come to. Maybe this is where the turkeys in my mom's yard always live. Perhaps this is where we all end up, or really, where we've been all along without realizing it, and it really takes a tragedy to make you see that words never really encompass us. They were never really part of any city of ours. What does this mean for me as a writer? Can I learn to write with something other than words? Is that what all the cooking is about? I think this city that transcends language may be where Leslie Booker is trying to direct me daily on my meditation app, this idea that we are in this ocean of language and moods and events and feelings and promotions and births and funerals, and we think all these things are us, but the whole time we have been the ocean. It's a worthy twist ending. Then, when I close my eyes this time, there it is: I see my father. He is, in fact, hustling people at pool, charming and wily as ever. He gives me this look like, *I'm all good and now it's time for you to go back to your own life.* I try to hold on, to grab a pool stick, but I see that it's time. I feel his love. I never want to leave the train where I found him, but leaving is part of the agreement. We reach Southeast.

We are all such haunted things. Protecting inner and outer frontiers at so much cost. The inner weather always shifting, the outer weather going wild in climate transformation. It's a wonder we can do things as sensible as go on job interviews, rub our sweaty palms against other sweaty palms like we're trying to make flame. Death has taught me the true architecture. Now, when I walk around Brooklyn, I imagine the roof and walls of all the apartment buildings removed, revealing the people crouched inside, trying to be people, so close to others while not realizing it, not actually alone. I picture, too, the bodies of the people on the streets this way, their skin pulled back like curtains, where I can witness the workings of what makes them, their most distant borders they vowed to show nobody, and even, yes, that piece that will one day bring them death, it's always there in life, hovering like my father's birthday king balloons, playing pool like my father is now, waiting to take us back. I don't fear it anymore, when I spot it beneath the skin curtains of the passersby, I wink, wave. I call it over to me. When it finally comes, bedraggled, I will take it into me as I've soothed my terrified children so many times by the smell of my skin alone.

37.

In art, we see this little play acted out between love, death, and despair, hope and acceptance over and over with no real—or known at least because it's impossible—resolution. What happened for my father when they put the fuchsia band on his wrist and turned his vitals screen, too, fuchsia? We only know my side of the story, what happened on this plane, but what fascinates me is what happened on his end. After the fact, my mother, ever the rampant eccentric, says she wishes she had taxidermy-style stuffed him so she could keep him with her always. *He was so quiet, anyway*, she says. My mother, the Norman Bates of Putnam County.

38.

But look, there do remain wondrous things worth struggling towards. The stories we hold close are about just this, and we are the characters who keep approaching these horizons, even through the dark bits, strange times and spaces and, in many of these tales, through death itself, to get there. We see in the end that we are the time machines. After he is cremated, weeks later we get up the guts to open the cardboard box they have sealed him in. We find ash. I was hoping there would be a Mary Shelley and Percy situation wherein some claim his heart didn't burn during cremation, so she kept it in her writing desk. Because my father wanted it this way, we never buried him. So I bury him here with you.

Acknowledgments

I am grateful to the *Kenyon Review*, which featured earlier versions of some of this material. I am thankful to T. Thilleman, Aurelia, and Spuyten Duyvil for making this book come to life.

I appreciate the patient and inspiring members of my little household, Adriel, Layla, and Max Gerard, for listening to me talk endlessly about this book and providing wise responses.

This book wouldn't have been written without the love and support (and childcare!) of my family, Trish and Louis Hagood (in the past), Judi Weinstock, Charley Gerard, Eva Gerard, and Phil Bender.

Thanks also to the family (and family friend) literary support of Kay Whitney, Natalie Hennessy, Heidi and Mike Bender, Joan Erskine, Sofia Zambenedetti, Ariel Zambenedetti, and Josephine Kuhl.

Thank you to the friends who come to every reading (or entertain my children so I can go): Miku Terai, Daniella Furman, Julie Mulligan, Julia Goldstein, Emily Bona-Cohen, Adrianne Fiala, Jill DiDonato, Jeanne Puchir, Kristen Puchir, Robert Puchir, Bret Puchir, David Coates, Rebecca Lehde Coates, Sagar and Jahnvi Shah.

It has been crucial to have the support of my Hanging Loose Press family: Joanna Fuhrman, Jiwon Choi, Mark Pawlak, Bob Hershon, Elizabeth Hershon, Donna Brook, Keri Smith, Thomas Moody, and Dick Lourie.

I wouldn't be here without those who supported my writing early on: Leonard Cassuto, Heather Dubrow, Sarah Gambito, Elisabeth Frost, Keri Walsh, Marty Skoble, Veronica Russo, Linda Greenberg, Marc Vincenz, Jennifer Ryan, Barish Ali, Peter Ramos, Karen Sands-O'Connor, Aimable Twagilimana.

Thanks to Elaine Equi, Idra Novey, Jiwon Choi, Ananda Lima, and Joanna Fuhrman for taking the time to read the book and say nice things about it.

I am glad to have such a great writing group, The Carroll Street Collective, and the support of Theo Gangi, Ian Maloney, Jason Dubrow, Emily Edwards, Jen Wingate, Athena Devlin, Mitch Levenberg, Jive Poetic, and Virginia Franklin in writing at St. Francis College.

I am so happy that my parents, Trish and Louis Hagood, encouraged me to be a writer given how uncertain that path is. Most of all, I hope that my father is reading this book somewhere…

CAROLINE HAGOOD is Assistant Professor of Literature, Writing and Publishing and Director of Undergraduate Writing at St. Francis College in Brooklyn. She is the author of two poetry books, *Lunatic Speaks* and *Making Maxine's Baby*, a book-length essay, *Ways of Looking at a Woman*, and *Weird Girls*, as well as the novel, *Ghosts of America*.